811.5
Sul

109478

Sullivan.
Incident in silver.

The Library

Nazareth College of Rochester, N. Y.

INCIDENT IN SILVER

Books by

A. M. SULLIVAN

Progression and Other Poems
Elbows of the Wind
New Jersey Hills
Ballad of a Man Named Smith
Ballad of John Castner
Day in Manhattan
Stars and Atoms Have No Size
Tim Murphy, Morgan Rifleman

Incident In Silver

A BOOK OF LYRICS

by

A. M. Sullivan

New York

The Declan X. McMullen Company, Inc.

1950

DISCARDED

NAZARETH COLLEGE LIBRARY

Copyright, 1950

by A. M. Sullivan

10 9478

Acknowledgment is made to *The Saturday Review of Literature, Catholic World, America, Spirit, Poetry, a Magazine of Verse, The Sign,* The New York *Times,* and the New York *Herald Tribune,* where many of these poems have appeared. The title poem is from *The Poetry Chapbook.* Several poems appear for the first time. A few others are reprinted from an earlier volume, *Elbows of the Wind.*

Printed in the U.S.A.

CONTENTS

811.5
Sul

In Memory of my Father
a story teller
who spun a bright fabric
of legend about the world
of his children and their
children

PILGRIM

Grass is tougher than steel,
The sod outwears the spade.
The road outruns the wheel,
The task outlives the trade.

Here where I swing the scythe
And call the hidden clover,
Earth asks the season's tithe
Before my labor's over.

Earth's beauty I have found
Twice beautiful for change,
And my ear upon the ground
Hears music old and strange.

Life's answers are the same,
The questions vary only,
Man writes an ancient name
But men are new and lonely.

What little I have learned
Has added to my lack,
For the road has always turned
And never once led back.

THE HIDDEN TREE

Under the gravel, rock and clay
The eyeless branches probe and creep,
Shouldering life and death away,
Drinking darkness, drinking deep.

The branches thirsting for the light
Trap the sun and moon and star,
Long arms enclose the day and night
And gather blossoms from afar.

The tree that earth and heaven made
Is all that dawn and darkness prove;
With the root sap flows the shade,
With the sunlight shadows move.

Light and darkness, drink them both;
The tree that anchors in the mind
Pries the rock to gather growth;
Wisdom borrows from the blind.

THE CANDLE AND THE COIN
(*After Blake*)

Rub your eyeballs and behold
The turmoil of the firmament,
And watch the galaxies unfold
In the blue light and the gold
Of error growing eloquent.

Brush the darkness from the soul
Ere the shadows leave their stain
Upon the edges of the scroll
Where conscience blundering like a mole
Blinks and measures its domain

Find the candle hid within
The twinkle of the morning star,
And visit with your kith and kin
For they have traveled from afar
To hear the whispering paladin.

Seize the coins of light that fall
Silent on the dusty floor
And hurl them over wisdom's wall
And when the blindmen shake the door
There will be light enough for all.

TIME'S PORTION

Against the dark square of tomorrow's window
Man holds his face and slowly blinks an eye
Only to find his nose pressed to a mirror
And the mirror clouded by a moment's sigh.

He dare not turn his head upon his shoulder
Lest creeping shadows make him cry aghast
Where the sun climbs up the cenotaph's high finger
And the shadow's finger points into the past.

Time has two hidden piles for him to conjure,
The spent and unspent, cleaving them with light
That marks the hour. Who can tell the measure,
The measure of the time piled out of sight?

MEASURE

There is a sound to measure planets by
When dusk unfolds the greater arc of sky;
Listen—the golden tread of light
Makes Time more audible in the still of night.

VILLANELLE OF LIGHT

Time is no measure, there is only light
To gauge the distance in the curve of dark
Man blinks and holds the heavens in his sight.

The window's square describes the width and height
Of starry acres, never the chimes' long arc.
Time is no measure, there is only light.

Love gauges shelter in the gloom of night
By roof and wall, and with the sulphur spark.
Man blinks and holds the heavens in his sight.

Hate measures hatred by the steel in flight
But time will play her treason. Despots, hark:
Time is no measure, there is only light.

The tree of faith forever burning bright
Will brand the shadows with its golden bark.
Man blinks and holds the heavens in his sight.

We count the pulse beats with a secret fright
And watch space dwindle to a granite mark.
Time is no measure, there is only light;
Man blinks and holds the heavens in his sight.

COUNSEL FOR YOUTH

Let not the white, hot metal of your desire
Chill under the breath of scorn;
Before the dream dies, gather the bitter briar
And watch the flames leap higher
Making a golden fagot of every thorn.

Drink your rapture before the blood thickens,
In bulging and brittle veins;
Sire your phantoms while the pulse quickens,
Else the spirit sickens
And the rainbow drips from unwoven skeins.

Fling your golden pennies to the intrepid dancers
Who spin on the point of swords,
And borrow the red shawl of the necromancers
Or all your lyric answers
Will crumble into words.

THOMAS SURRENDERS

A tranquil terror grips my soul;
No surly wind is stirring,
And silence perches on the knoll
Where savage doubts are purring.

No tocsin of a gallant foe
Shall echo from my cymbal;
Jehovah sheathes his sword, and lo,
I thumb a brassy thimble.

I crave the clangor of the steel
The sting of pike and sabre,
The blundering of the cannon-wheel
And Death's incessant labor,

But Peace comes with a coward's kiss
And tempts me with her silver,
Doubt signs the bloodless armistice,
My heart upon the salver.

THE POROUS PEOPLE

We are the porous people
Shot through by the hidden arrow,
And tipped with dawn or darkness
It passes through bone and marrow.

The darts of the Hertzian wave
Follow the rim of the planet
And burrow the land and water
And pry the veins of granite.

The light of the Roentgen eye
Is dark as the star of hate;
It reaves the ramparts of flesh
And burns on the silver plate.

Constant as rain are the lances
That lunge at the crust of earth,
Rays from the corners of chaos
Coming since Lucifer's birth.

For we are the porous people
Thinner than wind and the rain,
The rumors of war pass through us
And only the past is slain.

Pierced by the flying minute
That pauses once for death,
Our moments saddle the pulse
And ride to the end of breath.

OUT OF THE DEPTHS

When a thirst within the sky
Sucks the bed of ocean dry

The bottom of the sea
Will inform posterity

Of time's long inventory
Of the fruits of hate and glory

But now we ask no more
Than the driftwood on the shore

And the face of the troubled sea
Is anonymity.

SONG FOR PASSING YOUTH

Doomed is the tree
Where the dead leaf clings,
And life's feathers fall
From moulting wings.

When part of me dies
I cut the tether
And drop the leaf
And shed the feather.

Plucked of the plumage
That decked my youth,
The candid peacock
Bares the truth.

I clothe my pride
In homespuns, warm
Enough to shield me
From the storm,

And beg the word
Of praise to hold
In charity
Against the cold

And count my pulse
Against the thief
Of youth's red feather
And love's green leaf.

NOSTALGIA

There's a far-off look upon the faces
Of the strangers in the market places,

And eyes reach with the mind's eye
Over the transoms of the sky

And eyes speak with the heart's word,
And over the tumult love has heard

The lonely one, the eager one
Grow eloquent till light is gone,

Moving their lips with the moving crowd
But nothing is ever said aloud.

CALCULATION

God asleep is space
And God aroused is time;
The tides within the blood
Began at Eden's prime
And kept their even pace
With passion's wane and flood.

How shall we measure then
The inch the body takes
Or the orbit of the soul
When a voice within awakes
And asks of tired men
The distance to the goal?

The heavens bend from high,
Earth reaches from below,
And prayer and promise meet
In the wreath of cloud and snow,
Past oceans of the eye
And the mind's confusing street.

How far then have we come,
How far have we to go
Till the cry of love is heard,
And the eyes of faith shall know
That the grave is an empty home
And death is a foolish word?

GREEK LEGEND

The fox that gnaws your gut, O Spartan friend,
Will leave a void that conscience cannot fill
Nor thieves applaud since no man knows the end
To which a fox may go to serve him ill.

The fox that crawls beneath your ribs will eat
The eager heart and never taste the spleen,
For foxes relish all that love holds sweet
Till the pulse is quiet and tooth is clean.

Men hiding foxes speak a tongue perverse.
They ask an evil act of God, and pray:
"Turn something into nothing, like the curse
Within my breast that eats the soul away."

If you steal foxes, hold the beast aloft
In public crime and show the fangs of doubt,
And be less brave because the flesh is soft
And pride will never drive the vixen out.

PRISONERS

Man grows large and earth small
And his eyes reach and his elbows spark,
But he has never scaled the wall
To worlds that glisten after dark.

Earth holds him though his brain be clever
At fashioning fiery wheel or wing,
No iron cleat or pinion ever
Broke the night's invisible ring.

He searches earth and sky to find
A hidden door to the East or West,
Out of body and out of mind
But turns no knob within his breast.

His pride has wings but conscience shrinks
In the acid of the mind's pretense
And the lost soul of a Christian blinks
At the rumors of its innocence.

Man has less though much be taken
In heavy fruit from wisdom's seed,
The sweeter orchard of love's forsaken
In the quarrel of gnat and centipede.

Where shall he go? There is no other
World to which the fool may climb;
When shall he sit beside his brother
And share the little gift of time?

ADAM'S SONG

Stuff his ears with the alphabet
And cram his gut with numbers,
What can a vagrant of chaos get
When the soul of wisdom slumbers?

What shall it profit to save his soul
If the light of his soul is lost
And music is drained from a broken bowl
And the sweat of his brow is frost?

Open the sluice of the heavenly gate
With grace for the guttering wick;
Save him, O Christ, for the hour is late,
The spirit of man is sick.

CREDO

I believe in God the Father
Because He knows the vast
Pretensions of the atom,
And stare at Him aghast
As he cracks it in His knuckles
Twixt the present and the past
And sets my faith aflame
With Creation's mighty blast.

I believe in God the Son
Because I see His blood
Come spilling from a tree
And make a roaring flood
That drowns the world in love
Beneath the Holy Rood
Where the ebbtide sucks out evil
And the floodtide brings all good.

I believe in God the Spirit
Because when I was young
I found a wounded sparrow
Whose eager talons clung
To my fingers as I breathed
A prayer, half-said, half-sung,
And the sparrow's sudden pinions
Felt the fire of my tongue.

The Father, Son and Spirit,
All Power, Love and Grace—
The Triune rules the heavens
Wherein the angels trace
God's leash upon the creatures
That haunt the holy place
And the starlight burns with glory
In the wrinkles of His face.

SONG FOR THE YOUNG MEN

Sitting on the brink of chaos
The sad-eyed sibyls chant our doom;
What they sing shall not dismay us
Though a shadow grows and dwindles
With the anger of no answer.
Hope has built a sudden loom;
Faith has filled the seven spindles.
Ah, with light toes of the dancer
We shall race the perilous rim
Of the darkness, calling Him—
Calling Him whose voice we heard
Above the wailing of the sibyls;
Thunder stomps upon the trebles—
We have listened to the Word

THE MARCH

No generation's lost;
Earth is too small a place,
And Life too little time
For any man to boast
That he could turn his face
In Zero's pantomime.

The march of Pride began
At Eden's shattered gate
When Adam broke the pact
Between a God and man,
And though the hour is late
Pride justifies the act.

He bellows vain demands
Upon the stubborn lock
Of the door to Kingdom Come
And reaches with rude hands
Beneath the starry clock
To touch the pendulum,

And climbs the narrow wall
Of light that is Today
And half in scorn and sorrow
Looks backward at the shawl

That dims from gold to grey
Then schemes against Tomorrow.

He teeters on the ledge
Above the dark abyss
Where tumbling Lucifer
Betrayed an angel's pledge
And heard the serpent's hiss
"Hell hath no sepulchre."

The raiment of despair
Is chilling to the bone.
Shall pride in all his scorn
Ask nothing else to wear
And stand aloof, alone
And damned on Judgment Morn?

Pride will not be interred
Within the draughty skull
But preens enormous wings
In prismed light, a bird
That haunts the rookery, full
Of Adam's broken things.

Only the wilful blind
Go hooded after dawn
And bruise against the light.
They net the teasing wind

And when the game is done
Catch folly in its flight.

The generations come,
They go in dusty ranks;
Some tethered in a snare
Of Pride's cold vacuum;
Some free to give their thanks
Upon the evening stair.

Let Anger set the pace
Until the bugles cry
The hour of bivouac,
Love with a better grace
Will tell them where to lie
And close the almanac.

The generations march
Into the rising sun
And from the rebel horde
Pride storms the morning arch;
Before the day is done
Love bargains with the Lord.

No generation's lost
Though men have gone astray;
Pride bent beneath his load
Finds footprints in the frost,
His own from yesterday
Along the curving road.

CHOICE

There are two ways of going blind—
You have your choice and you may choose,
When there is nothing else to lose
But time and comfort of the mind,
To draw the shades and close the doors
And empty transoms of the light,
And darkness soaking through the pores
Will dull the retina with night.

Or you may find a quicker way,
The utter dark that heroes take
When honor has the choice to make
And who is there to answer nay?
They stare into the flaming disc
Knowing the battle must be won
When eyes of young men take the risk
And drain their sockets in the sun.

NIGHT GAZETEER

Night's curtain lifts from present to past,
The hours hang heavy upon the spangled shawl;
Breathless I rub the ceilings of the vast;
Informed of space, I never move at all.

Rising and falling across the window ledge,
Antares on the roof-tops is not far
Above the beacon by the city's edge
That winks a red eye to the passing star.

Now I am roused and eager for the going,
Prowling the darkness on the wings of light,
Guided by lanterns past the realms of knowing,
Sure of the way until the dawn's green blight.

To gather Chaos mark Orion's square
Within the pane; to find the rim of Order
Lift the sash and draw a dark line where
The planets roll along the jeweled border.

Out of the squinting windows of the skull
The caged mind measures the heaven's huge ellipse,
Plunging beyond eye-depth where skies grow dull
With Time's slow dust from the inaccessible crypts.

The light is flame, and I who probe the grate
Of worlds lost in the shaking cannot hinder
The birth of Hell's first atom; soon or late
It glows to fury, and dims in hate to cinder.

My little cry of anguish will be lost
In a windy maze, but not the brave endeavor
Of one bright match that blinks into a ghost
Before my breath, and joins the stars forever.

FISSION

Curious fingers probed the secret vault,
Pried the lid above creation's flame,
Reluctant Heaven gives neither praise nor blame
And men must choose the virtue or the fault.

AURORA BOREALIS

I

The show begins at half-past any hour
When curtains blowing in the spectral wind
Swing from casements opening in the north,
And from the dark lakes of the solar fires
Electrons move across night's pediment
Below the stars but high above the wall
That prisons man who lives by breath alone,
Whose heart is shaped by stones of gravity.

II

The parasol that spreads across the vault
Sways in the hands of a gymnast seeking balance
Who runs the tightrope strung from East to West
And we who stare and catch the ragged rainbow
Implore the dancer in her saraband
For the secret blossoms of the little worlds
That roll along the ribs of her umbrella
And dim the stars that swing around Polaris.

III

Slower than light but faster than the pulse
Sun's bullets burst to prisms in the sky

And the face of night glows with the fatal fever
Of a dying atom drained of hate and fury
And color falls upon the wincing eyes
With the sting of raindrops from the pointed eaves
Whose gutters drain into the vats of time.

GENESIS

The light is music, and the first note breaks
The shuttered silence like a bird in flight;
This is not morning but the end of night,
The long night when the urge for being aches
In Time's slow womb, and a windy rhythm shakes
The shadows from the sun, and from the height
And breadth of Heaven fades the sullen blight
Of emptiness and God in joy awakes.

The layers of aeons crumble from the dark
Stirred by the anthem of angelic strings
And Order comes with a lordly whirr of wings
And worlds are made in the expanding arc
Of splendor till a last note finds its mark
And Man spits out the primal clay and sings.

I

Laughter is our last resource since Anger fails
And gnashing of the teeth may scar the tongue;
Let us search the tribe and plumb the cavernous breast
For the feathery nest of nerves beneath the rib
And prod the source of song with a gentle finger.
If the lout shall sing till crystals of heaven quiver
Then know the hour has come to turn the glass
And twist the lip to the upper curve of laughter.

II

When the Almighty's happy bluster stirs the wind
To sudden loops of thunder along the hills,
Neither man nor beast shall tremble at His voice
But cry, "Hallelujah, Lord," to the beat of tocsin.
Let the lowly of heart discard the sad sweet echo
And dance on the drumheads, stretched over ribs of sorrow;
For laughter's a shield, and joy is a shining sword
To hurl at banners of hate in the gathering gloom.

III

The sunlight sprays through dusty groins on urns
And dances down bronze of braggarts in the tombs,
Or fingers the worthy names in chapel windows.
Honor the dead alone who died for honor,

And laugh as the Judas ram lies down to slaughter,
Shorn of his bell on the bloody altar stone.
The lambs shall paw the dawn in merry candor
And answer reveille with ironic bleat
Till battles of all the world are lost in laughter.

IV

Faith is the coin to spend in the nub of morning
When buds unfold a lip to drink the dew
And prayer is an angry bird to jar the shutter
By the attic stair where you lost a tarnished penny.
Pick up the coin again. Behold the image
And render to Caesar all if Caesar turns
A face of anger after the words you sing.
But if young Jesus smiles with the sun's medallion
Render to God a tithe for the gift of song.

ENCOUNTER WITH OBLIVION

No stomping ogre of the night
Can stun me with a blow
So horrible as the blight
Of emptiness I know.

Ghosts, in youth I knew them
And was by ghosts befriended;
Griffons I met and slew them
And demons I defended.

But the nameless taunt that stared
From a gaping red socket
Left me too scared
To challenge or mock it.

If ever a fiend or beast
Pursues me to the dawn,
There are mad eyes at least
For one to look upon,

But smoking nausea of space
Creeps from a hollow mask—
Once, I have seen this face
But never again I'll ask.

If God alone is prime,
The essence of all good,
I saw pure evil climb
Out of the shadowy hood

And I stripped the dewy shawl
With fingers tense and numb
And then uncovered all
Of a spirit's vacuum.

WARNING

What festers in the skulls of men who walk
The city streets as if their minds were fleeing
Dark birds of prey that spin about their being?
What is it clouds their reason as they talk
A pattern of sound as aimless as the chalk
Marks of a child? There is no word for freeing
These captives of the brain—no veil from seeing
The curved beak of the harpy and hawk.

If thought made visible on the fevered lip—
If thought made terrible in the drooling jaw
Turns the bright mask of wisdom into pain,
Behold no muttering mouth today, but grip
The knob of reason lest some canker gnaw
A hole into the thin door of your brain.

THE WIND

I

A tree writhes in a windy torment
And the long roots clutch the anchoring stone;
A loose slate skids down a perilous angle
And shatters on the mossy flags of the court;
An old man leans against the flume of air
And his cheeks redden with rasp of the season.

The invisible substance of the wind sifts upward
Arching a pliant roof for the world—
Blue roof high as a frescoed ceiling
Grey roof lower than the gable cock
Gold roof fragile with the glitter of dusk
When the spectrum tilts and the vials tumble
And the day sky splinters with the falling sun.

There's fuel for the blood in the frosty air
When the lungs are stoking cold bubbles of dawn
And the pulse hammers hard to a hornpipe rhythm
And the heels scuff silver from October grass.

By what shrewd knavery on an autumn day
Are four winds mixed to a drowsy calm?
The hawk treads up the staircase of noon
And his shadow blurs in the meadow haze.

The honey bees traffic at the cider press
And drink their fill from the heady pulp.

II

Once Icarus fell in the blue Aegean
As he reached for the fringe of the golden fleece,
And closed wet fists on the raveling edge.
Leonardo looked to the Ligurian Sea
And plumbed the cubic acres of sky
Where the great storks flew to the Moorish vanes.
His left hand dropped the sinister brush
And he set his calipers on the heft of the wind.

Hope running on tiptoe down Kitty Hawk dunes
Swung a lasso that caught the mane of the wind
And man kicked loose from the long grip of earth.

III

When fingers of dynamite pry veins of the boulder
The hurt hill trembles and the windows rattle
And sound walks backward on the plateaus of air,
Stumbling to silence in the cushioning glens.
The growl of the cannon is racing the ball
Hurled over the map to frighten a neighbor,

But iron is swift and death has the answer
When the voice of anger lags on the wind.

Time on the slope is skirling his pipes
And the blare of the drones is webbed in the winds
As the bivouac shakes the shadows of fear—
Fontenoy, Balaklava, Gettysburg,
Verdun, Bastogne, Iwo Jima;
The farm boy drops his sickle to listen.

IV

Since the chorus of Sophocles sang
By the cool grove of Tempe
Or shorn maids of Carthage twisted hair into hawsers,
Grief's fingers have plucked the strings of the wind.

Forever the chant of the Psalms
Is drumming on clapboards of Heaven
And kites flutter up to the high throne of Mary
Bearing "Ora pro nobis," and "Salve Regina,"
As the long spool of praise unwinds in a prayer never
    ending
For the sky is no further than weighted winds
Will carry the cry "Hosanna."

PSALM AGAINST THE DARKNESS

What shall we fear, son, now that the stars go down and silence
is chilling the breath to a pattern of frost?

Stalactites glisten from caverns of night for the grief of the
world is hardened again into swords.

Cankers of malice are boring their icy augers deep in the bosoms
of men, and the hooves of the four horsemen are heard on
the roofs of the brain

What is this prescience of doom, this stalk of evil that sucks the
sap of the spirit, and spreads the pollen of anger?

Some witch is abroad in the world paroled for an hour of mischief to scatter her cockle in furrows of hope.

We have taken the earth in our stride, but the boot is crusted
in clay, and the cleat has bruised the dream bogged low in
the darkness.

Heads downward, we count the treadmill steps to the sky in
a litany mixed with a laugh and wordy bluster of braggarts.

II

Standing on the rim of the world we beat hollow drums in our breasts, we shout into caverns a challenge of God

Nimble are we in the centuries to alter our skin, our tongue and our shrine, but never the bloody oblation as Abraham also remembered.

Peace, peace, we cry, till our voice is shrilled to a paean, but map men wrangle by mountain and river

Knowledge we gather as a conquering host, and pile the loot of the years in bins of oak and of marble, but wisdom we cannot bequeath.

The heat of blood is the same as the night it spilled on the lichened rocks in a world too small for the fingers of Cain.

III

Which is more difficult, son, to save the world, or end it swift in a vacuum, sans mark or memory of men?

What is the goal of the centaur whose fingers have changed the wine of Cana to gall, who sold his art to Magus and fouled the steps of the temple?

What shall we fear too much? Hate's guarantee of our doom?
    Love's indestructible dawn? The half-god who stumbles
    on pride cannot end his world by the wishing.

A finger rising from conscience and shadowing the sun shall
    mark the hour with less than His praise, yet curve a rain-
    bow high over Golgotha.

The finger has written again on the curved deception of blue,
    and the words are the old, old cry of "Eli, Eli, lama
    sabactani."

IV

There are two majorities, son, though you ask me no question.
    The nameless dead, the unborn legions of time, but we are
    the thin minority, the living, who hold the sceptre of light.

Music distills the heavy mist of rapture
In the phantom sky, and on the flood
Of sound we sally forth to capture
The substance of a mood.

If there be one still greater than the bard
Who gave the first wild word a wing,
It would be him who chilled the metal hard
And made it sing,

Or him who stretched the gut of Egypt's cow
Across the viol's clumsy wound,
Making a throat for pain, so that his bow
Commanded sound—

Sound that feathered the spirit's pinions
And struck the flinty heart to fire.
Swords may mark the conquered earth's dominions
But the reed and lyre

Have no sharp boundaries for our measure;
The timeless orbit of a song
Is traced by silver echoes and our pleasure
Is infinitely long.

Rob man of speech. Let him be ever dumb,
The loss of words will never matter much

Unless the strings upon his heart are numb
At music's touch.

It is not far from alpha to omega
But our mad hopes can scale the minaret
Upon the eight notes leading beyond Vega,
And any alphabet.

THE CIRCLE

World of incredible vistas, man has risen
Buoyant upon a dream till he uncovered
The blue and secret pattern of his prison.
Caged by a curve unending he has hovered
Above the crevices of dawn—saw dusk
Come billowing down the cataracts of gloom
And spread his nostrils wide to drink the musk
From a starry trellis in the darkened room.

Noon has a bright deception. We behold
The plausible arcs of azure where he soars
Like a worried wasp above the checkered wold.
He seeks a way to Heaven but the doors
Open on new horizons. Let him enter
And find himself still winging at the center.

SYMBOLS FOR DECEIT

Above the grassy lure
Of the quicksands
I build my house
Upon stilts of logic.

Fool's gold
Is minted by the moon
Amid the gurgle of spring tides
In the marshes.

Mirrors are smashed by pebbles
Dropped by gulls,
And where they fall
Is the throat of a whirlpool.

My mansion sags to the northward,
Its legs gnawed thin by doubt
And burdened by the weight
Of conscience.

Does my house lean
Wrong-angled against the evening?
It is shouldering the wind
Which bears a knapsack of anger.

A bird with a bloody beak
Has made a nest in the eaves.
She is hatching a prayer
Without wings.

REFLECTION

The monkey being angry at the game
Looks back of panels for the knave
That bares his teeth.
Had he but smiled
Ten thousand years of folly
Would have vanished from the glass.

NOVEMBER AFTERNOON

Fountains of light are lifting bubbles
On the white clapboards of the house
And the mouse
In the cool crevice of the eaves
Drags a sharp shadow
Over the window sill.

Leaf mould on the frosty floor of the forest
Is fool's gold in the angled glare
Of the afternoon
And tatters of sunlight tangle
In branches of birch and alder.

Skeletons grow luminous
And touch stiff fingers in the wind,
Light is the only living thing
Dancing amid dead leaves.

Black water refuses the color of sky
Till the dazzling eye on the mountain
Sets the lake afire
And silver fins shimmer in sudden schools
That dim beneath the swift cover
Of darkness rolling over.

The afterglow sifts down from a pink shroud
On the empty nest
And bargains briefly with the night
Amid the loud jargon of the crows.

HERITAGE

Where water folds across the stones
A kid glove over knuckle bones

And idles into pools, the trout
Lifts his speckled body out

Once, twice, and thrice he hurls
A whip of steel against the swirls,

Then leaps the rapids, and in air
Curves a note of music there

And with a swift contrary will
Climbs the staircase of the hill.

INCIDENT IN SILVER

The trees on the rim of the mountain
Stood stark in the lifting light
That spilled from the hidden fountain
Where the withered grass turned white;

Turned white and the sequins glistened
On the robe spread over the ground;
Something stirred and I listened,
Listened, and heard no sound.

Then the hour in the village struck
As I watched the full moon climb,
And I saw the head of a buck,
His antlers covered in rime.

The moon, the frost, and the deer
And I were caught in the spell
In the silver month of the year,
In the silver sound of a bell.

The clouds came over to staunch
The light that the moon had lost
And the buck with the silvery branch
Raced a shadow over the frost.

AFTER THE ICE STORM

Under the blue sky made bluer by the whiteness of the hills,
    the multitudes of the wind jostle the broken arms
    of the birches.

And not a cloud rides with them, only anguish in the arched
    radiance of the morning as a sapling strains in the
    shining surface of evil.

There is a noise in the forest where sound rushes
    through paths burrowed by invisible rogues of the
    bitter air,

And Death dancing and jubilant flaunts his jewels
    prismed on arms of skeletons
    writhing in sunlight.

No bird moves but the plumed dervishes
    clamber the icy walls, and the brief blemish of the
    deer tracks is lost in shifting veils.

A train whistle, lost in the valley, stumbles along the
    glazed granite and dies in the lap
    of the wind.

NAZARETH COLLEGE LIBRARY

IMMINENCE

The fox, the deer and grouse
Are never far away
Upon a winter's day
From the shadow of my house.

They listen for the boot
That breaks the crust of snow
And never turn to go
Till I am in pursuit.

I trail the patient fox
Without a dog or gun
But lose the wily one
In the wall of naked rocks.

I follow the tardy doe
Who pauses once to look
Before she leaps the brook
Of black water and blue snow.

The grouse against the light
Becomes a mottled stone;
I never would have known
Had she not taken flight.

The grouse, the fox and deer
Beneath the shadow's cover
Come back again and hover
By the thing they love and fear.

THE SEED

What tilted Apgar's old red barn this spring?
A very little thing to hear him tell;
He swept a bag of hay seed down a hole
In the sagging floor. Then came the thunderstorm
And the water crawled beneath the planks, a mole
Who probed the darkness with a silent knife.
The rafters creaked as seeds began to swell
And a million little giants came to life
And the old barn raised a corner to the west.
That's Apgar's story; the one I like the best.

NIGHT SONG

Cold water boils
In pools where the moonlight bubbles
And colder vapor coils
On paths where the bullfrog troubles
The things that fly, and creep—
Seeking sleep.

Blue shadows turn
Slowly in the spume of the shallow
And white meadows burn
With light of ghostly tallow
And the mallard in the brake
Is still awake.

But the quiet drifts
Down as the great cloud covers
The moon, and sifts
Silence over strangers and lovers
And never a sound is heard
From frog or bird.

VILLANELLE FOR JANUARY NIGHT

Tongues of the wind have buffed the furthest star,
The winter lakes chip crystal toward the moon;
Lonely and cold the light that comes afar.

The cloudy gates at midnight swing ajar,
The forest fingers strum a bitter tune,
Tongues of the wind have buffed the furthest star.

The sudden phantoms of the snowdrifts are
Enveiled in prisms on the snowy dune,
Lonely and cold the light that comes afar.

The lake explodes and silence wears a scar
Jagged with echoes where the dancers swoon,
Tongues of the wind have buffed the furthest star.

High on the elm, the hoot owls' voices mar
The spell of quiet with its frosty boon,
Lonely and cold the light that comes afar.

Lean daggers dangle from the jeweled spar
Of oak trees burdened since the thaw of noon,
Tongues of the wind have buffed the furthest star,
Lonely and cold the light that comes afar.

FIRST FREEZE

The roof of the morning crashes with a shatter of glass
As the brackish waters race with the call of the moon
And thin panes whiten and fall against rigid reeds.
Bells of frost tinkle above the muskrat's soggy door
And the white gull stands unseen in the white shards of the
    meadow,
Dry stalks nod and whisper in the snowy sedge
And the far off whistle is a jet of steam in the air
Before the voice of the engine rides from the river bridge.

The tide returning will not mend the roof of the meadow
But glaziers of the wind will stiffen the lapping water
With frosty needles that dart from the tufts of saw grass
And a sudden ceiling will sweep over the ears of the muskrat
And hold the tide in the hardening lid of the silence.

AT MIDNIGHT

As over the mountain's bulk Antares swung
In a golden parachute, and down the sky
Silence and the high winds buffed the stars,
There came the buck's long cry,

And then the voweled running call of dogs
Following the deer along the mossy ledge;
Night roused upon its haunches at the call
Of anguish at the onyx edge

As thin hooves pawed the air like rapiers
Lunging with futile thrust against the pack
Whose savage song pitched higher with the quarry
Caught in the starry cul-de-sac.

SUMMER RAIN

The soggy wind dies breathless amid the whisper of leaves
As the valley lost in the darkness awakens lost in the light.
The soft rain washes the pollen down the dusty sluices of corn
And sparrows splash in the puddles under steaming flanks of
    the mare
And worms in the morning riot through swelling sponges of
    lawn.
The sheep dog crashing the brush rouses a covey of quail
Who shatter the dawn's wet curtain with rapid thunder of
    wings.
The man who climbs in the wagon lifts a shining face toward
    the house,
One raindrop chasing another through the seven wrinkles
    of laughter.
Green is the color of joy where the timothy raises its banner
Beckoning to rabbits in warrens beside the field-stone fence.
Dark is the color of sound where the sentinel circles the elm
But the thrush makes a prism of song whistling its way to
    the meadow.
Grey is the color of peace where the heavens sag on the hills,

And the four ends of earth are a house, a barn, a tree and the
   haycock,
And the fullness of summer hangs on aching arms in the
   orchard.
Water gurgles and burrows from the spout by the kitchen
   window,
And water dripping from eaves jigs merrily over the flags
For this is the morning of rain and the end of thirst in the
   valley.

IN PRAISE OF EARTHWORMS

Earth breathes their glory through ten thousand pores,
Chimneys for summer's smithy in the sod
Where forges flourish in warm corridors
And commerce thrives beneath the thunderous plod
Of horses kicking the wet loam in the dawn.
After the rain they etch on steaming flags
Their ancient symbols, and build upon the lawn
The yellow mounds from which the prophet drags
His tardy inches and whispers through the land,
"Life is renewed," for this is Lesson Prime
In Genesis when the unpracticed Hand
Stretched clay to life, and life as long as time.

BLACKBERRY DREAM

My sleep is haunted by blackberries when the hours of picking
are over,

Dew-fed, sun-sweetened, they hang in the shadowy groins
of a chapel,

Where the light is prismed and sprayed by the gothic art of
a spider,

New canes with venomous briars strike with the spurs of a
gamecock,

And the trickle of sweat burns down the bloody ridge of the
scratches,

A green snake friendly and small swings on a stalk in the
thicket,

His curved head swaying in rhythm of hand and wrist to the
bucket.

A cat-bird circles and scolds and brushes my cap with a feather,

Her nest in the wild cherry crotch is veiled by the tentworm's
weaving.

The large berries purple and swell beyond the touch of my
fingers;

I stretch for the highest cluster, and step in a ground hog's
burrow,

Spilling the dark-rimmed treasure in the thorny maze of my
anquish.

Hands smarting in anger, I waken and smile at the tricks of
the daemon.

The walls of the darkness are crowded with wraiths who walk
to the kitchen,

And empty their pails and search for culls in a bustle of silence,
Till dimensions dim to a plane at the perilous edge of the
   pillow
And the blackberries dangle and fall beyond the reach of a
   dreamer
As languor seeps in the mind and drowns the light's last
   phantom.

DESERTED FARM

April renews the tedious duel
When the laggard fights the soil.
Each rising sun unfolds the cruel
Green challenge to the day of toil.
A faint heart strives upon the fields
That are not tamed by steel or time,
And when at last the coward yields
And quits the battle in his prime,
The nimble fingers of the season
Button a green coat over the brown,
And pity makes a pact with treason
To take a soiled flag back to town.

AFTER THE FOREST FIRE

After the red scourge whips through the forest and the cry
of anguish strangles in the dusk

Bent candles drip flame on the hill, grotesques in the orgy
of light.

At dawn the black buzzards rip their beaks in the haunch
of venison burned to a crisp in the thicket

And the carpet of silence rolls sombre and grey across the
lost whispers of noon.

Grey whorls of ash pirouette, wraiths of the trees in the
humorless taunts of the wind.

Lost is the hare who bounded beside the fox from the fangs of
a creeping dragon

Lost is the drumming of wings where the eggs of the pheasant
are boiled in the heart of an oak stump,

Lost is the swing of the gymnasts who bickered high in the
branches of the butternut and the shellbark.

Silence has seared all song in the mulch of the forest, stifling
the voice of the hour and season.

No hurt is as deep as the dagger of flame at the throat of the
beast and the root of the flower;

Tall oaks remember the season of pain for the saplings
withered around them,

Remember the blemish of fire when hate threw a torch in the
teeth of the wind and branded a mountain.

LATE AUTUMN

The falling leaf betrays the fawn
Standing rigid by the oak;
The wind that rises in the dawn
Blows away the meadow smoke
And frames against a greening sky
The mallard in the fowler's sight;
New tracks on hoarfrost publish why
The beagles yelp with young delight,
And early snow abets the treason
No words of pity may atone,
For Nature has a bitter season
When she informs upon her own.

PLENITUDE

Summer is come. The beetle's wings
Glint in the sun, and the wild thrush sings.

The bees go roistering through the vale
And stagger back with their heather ale.

Nature, drowsing upon the Earth,
Sighs with the generous pangs of birth.

Fruit on the tree, and fruit in the womb
Of the woman who peers from the shuttered room.

But Farmer John is worrying more
About the sow, and the ribboned boar,

And not the woman who counts the weeks
With the pallor of birth upon her cheeks.

Harvest is come. The barn is full;
The bleating ewes have lost their wool.

The old cow broods above her cud
Where the farmer spilled her bullock's blood.

The orchard and the arbor vine
Have brought him purple and amber wine

But bitter the taste of the wine of life
That burns in the veins of the farmer's wife.

The cow gave a calf that sold for a groat,
The sow brought a profit in each little shoat;

He bargained the colt of his Percheron mare
For a second-hand auto down at the Fair.

All bore their tribute, excepting his bride
Who came to travail and quietly died.

Winter is come. The shivering crow
Clings to the cross in the mound of snow.

QUATRAIN

When cockerels sparring at the fence
Fill the dawn with angry talk
The sudden shadow of the hawk
Postpones the private difference.

THE RETURN

Once when I spoke within the darkened stable
With teeth that chattered as the frantic words
Went fluttering to the hayloft and the gable
Like frightened birds

There was a phantom who would always greet
Me from some recess behind an oaken rafter;
Fancy and panic were rivals for my feet,
And a coward's laughter

Died in a gasp at my incarnate fear
Of the green eyes burning in the awful dark.
The cat would purr, and I could hear
The mournful bark

Of beagles and the soft bleat of the ewes.
Last night I went there once again to boast
But there was no disturbing news
From the haymow ghost

Nor friendly pawing from a stallion's hoof
Nor cat-eyes flashing jewels on the sable—
Only the moon dust sifting through the roof
Of the empty stable.

TO A DRYAD

A timid centaur paws the fragrant turf
Outside your woodland temple; nostrils steam
The frosty air like phantoms of the surf
That tumbles on the margin of a dream.
He is afraid, but fear is chained by awe
Of your frail splendor and your singing pride.
The half-beast lingers, bridle on his jaw
And eager for the spurs upon his hide.

But if you do not answer to his neighing
The creature of your tyranny will speak
The language of the higher brute, dismaying
Your ears with empty words, until a shriek
Will end the dream. And you will find me there
Embarrassed by the hoofprints on the stair.

MONUMENT

It was a mischievous wind that pushed him; a murderous gust
that jarred young Jan from the scaffold.

He teetered and swayed a hundred feet from the river over
weirs of iron and concrete.

Jan clawed at the wind but the assassin slipped through his
fingers and raced down the catwalk.

Jan reached for a cloud, for the horizon's thin line, for the
wing of a gull that leaned on the air.

The river paused at the cofferdam, fumed at the gorge, and
boiled through the tunnels of iron,

And a thousand men at their jobs saw a shadow that brushed
the wires and rigging around them.

Jan fell like a tumbling mallard, splashed in puddles of concrete, a spine of steel in his liver.

Jan's hat was a trophy of thieves, tossed and spun in gullies
of air, white buttons dancing in sunlight.

But Jan was smothered unseen in a vomit of stone that poured
from the lip of the flume,

And the lime in his bone was one with the lime that came
from the heart of the mountain.

Water and blood were welded to stone as the breath of Jan
rose high in a rainbow bubble,

And the bubble burst with the loosened spirit that raced from
darkness hardening around him.

The rigor of death was matched with the rigor of stone ere
they found Jan's hat by the river.

Rivers have flown by the tombs of the kings: the Nile,
Euphrates, the Tiber, Yangtse, and Thames.

No king has a tomb so great as the tomb of Jan who was
hurled from his throne by knaves of the wind.

Rich is Jan in the vastness hovering about him, the starry
vault of the hills, the cool lake pressing against him.

No ghoul shall enter his tomb for the Union card, the pocket
knife, and the new St. Christopher's medal.

No roar of the water in the turbines shall rouse King Jan in
the solemn depth of his slumber.

No wail of the ghosts in the windy gorge shall probe to the
ears that are sealed with the weight of a stone,

His mouth is gagged with the silence till the blast of a trumpet
high on the ledges of heaven

Pounds the tombs of the world into dust and loosens the dust
of Jan who sleeps with his back to the river.

FREE BURIAL

A pine box on a truck, the cortege came;
The wards of pity followed to the mound.
They stared in silence at the broken ground
And heard the silence broken by a name.

The old men bore their burden twenty paces
Nor paused to hear the muffled public prayer
And not a sob was stifled anywhere
Though anguish hung upon the wizened faces.

While bearers stumbled with the awkward freight
The driver of the truck dozed by the door,
"The Lord's my Shepherd" . . . He heard the thing before
And a stub cigar drooped with its soggy weight.

Ten yards away along Death's formal aisle
A man with bar and pick and shining spade
Cursed at a rock and the trouble that it made
And cursed again and threw it on the pile.

The driver roused, looked at the man and said:
"Another one today?" The digger shook
Clay from the shovel, knocked his pipe and took
His time to answer. "No one else is dead,

At least not now, but, son, it won't be long.
Three every month, and that's a steady rate.
Potter's Field is a place to speculate,
No empty holes." He laughed, "You can't go wrong."

The truck jarred into gear. "Son, what's your rush?
I'll save a place for you. Eat on the county
And sleep upon it too at public bounty.
It ain't so bad to lay your head on plush."

The digger wiped his muddy shoes, and when
The scraping tongues of shovels ceased their talk,
He joined the mourners coming down the walk
And the driver lit his soggy stub again.

SEARCH

There's little to say that hasn't been said
But the old, old story of love and bread,
And the infinite sky, the indefinite sea,
And the womb and the tomb's immensity.

CHRISTMAS UP-TO-DATE

The scribe and holy Pharisee
Buy the largest Christmas tree.

The windows of the high priest's home
Spot the snow in polychrome.

And Judas hangs a crimson wreath
With words of silver underneath.

And Pilate sends a greeting card
To all the rabble in the yard.

Salome dances till the dawn
And holds the foolish head of John.

The three wise men who traveled far
Are tipsy in the Pullman car.

King Herod has no lust for gore;
He owns a huge department store.

While every hostelry in town
Wears a brilliant Christmas gown,

A thousand Marys lie in pain,
A thousand Christs are born in vain.

And every vacant room is priced
To bar the coming of the Christ,

And scribe and holy Pharisee
Trim the largest Christmas tree.

DAWN MUSIC

The lookout in the branches
Keeps the vigil for the sun
And as the east sky blanches
He summons the feathery one
Drowsing in tall spires
With the whistling cry of "light,"
And the twittering of the choirs
Ends the dynasty of night.
After the solemn hush
Comes the hymn of day again
From the robin, finch and thrush,
The oriole and wren,
And the air is full of talk
From the crow who cannot sing
But the shadow of the hawk
Drops in silence from the wing.

DIAMOND DRILL

Boring vertically through time and rock
We sample a million years of earth's adventures
And with the jeweled fang of steel unlock
The secrets written in the hearts of stone
And learn today what time has always known
And whether a mining syndicate's debentures
Are worth their fractions in the daily paper.
The hollow tooth reveals its glinting core
To men who read its scientific lore
Like editors before the ticker tape
With news of fire and flood and every earthly caper
Before hot meadows shrank beneath the ice,
And hill and valley wrinkled into shape.
But we were probing down for iron ore;
Well, there it is, wedged in between the gneiss
At fifteen hundred feet, and the granite floor,
Triassic is the hour upon the clock.
The vein is hematite, and twelve feet wide
And far removed from blasting powder's knock.
There's many a shelf of limestone to be pried
As we sink an angled shaft through Cambrian time,
Some seventy million years, and it will cost
One hundred thousand dollars—just a dime
For each millennium. If risked and lost
In a war of metals come to sudden end,

Why worry, since men in their malice spend
All gold and silver first, and iron last;
And when the weight of ingots has been hurled
Over the roofs of foeman round the world,
The children of the dawn will stand aghast
At the cost per ton of final victory,
At the price per death for every warrior slain.
Yet, where the piedmont rises from the sea
The drills will burrow through the ancient crust
For treasures of tomorrow that remain
Hidden in earth's deep heart, while snow and rain
Devour bits of shrapnel in slow rust.

COMPENSATION

The seed of life is ever in the womb of death;
    Something must die that something shall be born.
You can hear the first gasp and the last faint breath
    Whenever a new page is added for an old leaf torn.

THE HAMMER

It's as simple as this: a pencil mark,
A head of steel on a hickory stick,
A tenpenny nail, and then the quick
Lift of the hand and the falling arc.

That's all there is. Primal force
In the hinged lever as the elbow bends,
A glint of light as the stroke ends
Unerring from the muscled source.

Through arid veins the probing nail
Spreads the oak grain, stops half-riven;
A second stroke, and the metal's driven
Through the board. If it should fail

And spoil the metal, blemish wood,
There is no way to mend the flaw
But turn the hammer, catch the claw
And draw the bad nail's twisted hood.

Momentum rides with the falling hammer,
Gives impetus to the binding fang
While cities rise with a loud bang bang
And men add cubits amid the clamor.

Though cities rise and fall, the sound
Lives longer than the tree and spike
And love and hate and envy strike
With hammers that echo on Calvary's mound.

THE KITE

The kite rides the waves of the treacherous wind
Breasting the breakers with a dolphin's grace,
Lifting over chimneys and dark water towers,
Dancing in the haze with the bright pretense
That freedom rides at the end of a string.
A lad's tall eyes climb the brick horizon
Past realms of the pigeons, and the lofty scowl
Of the warehouse windows where the shadows creep,
But the wind is frivolous and the stagnant air
Wraps the flag on the belfry in a deathly drape
And the kite sags down in the wind's deceit
A dolphin trapped in a weir of copper
Tossing its tail in a venomous gust
While the lad rolls string, and measures his grief
From the height of the curb to a starling's perch.

JET PLANE

Stung by the tail of a scorpion
Gravity loosens its grip
On the hide of a hellion
Who scorches the sky
Through a curve of silence
While sound is a laggard
In the tangled air.

The monster with open mouth
Sucks food from runnels of light
Washing blue space
Through a furious gut.

Tiptoe on the flattened world
The watchers are asking their eyes
If a dragon that swallows flame
Can burrow a hole
In the sagging roof of the morning.

Upon a ladder of smoke
The monster touches the zenith
But gravity roused from its spell
Reaches toward rafters of sunlight
And drags the scorpion down
To a crevice of earth.

THE TRYSTING

Here where the starlight filters on the ground
Is the only place where clay and phantom meet;
Your sandals make no impress and no sound
But the lawn must wear the bruises of my feet.

The fountain breaks the water into bits
Of silver echoes, muffled in the dark;
A lightning-bug darts through the elm and slits
Her purple tunic with his sudden spark.

Your one dimension challenges my three;
Proud reason gropes and taunts my certain faith
That love could ever bring you back to me
But you have come—how shall I greet a wraith?

A note of laughter dancing down the lane
Has scarred the silence. Through the breathing wood
Lean daggers pierce the ribs of trees and stain
The sylvan palace with a yellow flood.

The gay marauders halt before the gate
And sense the warning of your sentinel
Who keeps our little grove inviolate
Lest vagrant words might break the fragile spell.

Life is more strange than Death upon the lawn;
But have no fear, the alien voices fade
And we shall sit in reverie till the dawn
Peers up the slope and flaunts his gold cockade.

SEA SONNET

Life breaks about us in a charmed white hour
With the happy hazard love has always found
Upon a headland amid the clamorous sound
Of wind and water. Enchanted by the power
Of sinewed surf we watch the tide devour
The ribbon of sand; now briny sea fists pound
The jutting jaw of stone, and all around
Us blooms the rainbow's momentary flower.

Flood tide creeps in our thirsting veins. How soon
It surges across the jetties of a vow
Lifting our hearts, long beached upon a dune
Of pride. Forget the arid years; for now
The distant coaster smudging the azure noon
Shall carry our love on a swift and golden prow.

VIGIL

We waited for the visitor to come;
We listened for the fingers at the lock;
Life clung to the swinging pendulum
Losing rhythm with the tick of the clock.

Seconds dripped like the water from a tap,
And the tides of the blood came to ebb,
Let him call, let him speak, let him rap,
For a soul wrangles loose from its web.

We were waiting for a foe and a friend,
The foe and the friend, they were one.
We could bargain with a foe to the end,
But the friend cast his mantle on the sun.

An eye lost the light of the morning,
A voice lost the bright ring of gold,
And then came the blue shadow's warning,
And the wind and the shadow were cold.

Though his touch was soft as a feather,
Though his word came as silent as the frost,
His sword swept clean through the tether
That binds up the clay and the ghost.

We paused when the visitor was gone,
Paying homage to a sovereign and a thief,
None asked him for respite, there was none
But he gave us a long day of grief.

SHADOWS ARE BLACK

Shadows are such knavish things
They revel in the dawn,
And when the haughty bluebird sings
They stretch across the lawn;
But how the little vagrants run
Before the golden spears of sun.

Shadows are not holy things,
But fragments of the night.
They flit about on ebon wings,
While angels wear them white.
At dusk they leave the choir stalls
And fly across cathedral walls.

Shadows are quite awkward things.
They bend and twist askew.
Nor have they lovely colorings
Like woodland flowers ... even you
Who wear the rainbow on your back
Must have a shadow that is black.

LATE ENCOUNTER

I

What I have to say is not said with the curve and the flowing
Of speech of one whose lips make a bubble of song
But the blurt and the wrangle of sound from the breast of
a child
Who was hurt by the frost of the morning and scourge of
the wind,
Whose tongue was lamed by the blemish of words that were
spoken.
I have sought to name the things that prod me with anger,
The spur and the cleat that bruise the tissue of dreams,
But they dart with the dawn through walls that are chinked
with the looting,
Porous as combs of the bees, and damp with the flavor of honey;
And sweetness and venom drip back on the wounds of my
tongue.

II

The sluggard at dawn awakes and dimly remembers
The scamper of heels in the darkening attic of song.
Were they words of the rebel soon maimed by the kick of the
coward?
Were they the mice of the mind that nibbled the edges of
wisdom?

I have heard the scuffle of rhymes, the endless clawing of
     questions,
And the whimper of hopes long sealed in the bins of my youth.
I am troubled with time and the days that I marked for
     plowing,
For darkness is come and the seeds that were mine for the
     furrow
Are strewn on the curves of the wind, in the frown on the
     cliff and the crevice,
Rooted to flourish in sunlight and drain the sap of a
     moment.

III

Now I drop my acorn at dusk in a meadow swept by a circle
And the dew shall waken the giant who sleeps in the walls
     of the seed
And he'll leap again for the sky in the tardy lunge of the
     seasons
And bundle his brawn on the boughs to wait the call of the
     birds.
While his shadow shall frolic in the lengthening leash of
     the twilight,
His root shall search in my soul for the fading color of
     sound.

LITANY FOR MOUNTAIN CLIMBERS

Against the bleak solace of a gauge
Against the blue weight of the sky
Against the chisels of the wind
Honed by malice to a bitter edge,
Against the loud drumming of the heart
Against the cry of forfeit in the lungs
Against the faint whimper of reason
Let us climb for the joy of numbers
And add slow cubits to our size.

Like children learning to count aloud
Like idiots reaching to pluck a star
Like pedlars asking a martyr's pack
And the leashes of a tyrant will,
Like Satan shivering upon the height
And none to tempt with pride's cold plunder
Let us tilt our spines to the mountain's angle
And sink our spikes in the glacier's brow.

Under the dark wrinkles of the Matterhorn
Under the smooth cheek of the Jungfrau
Under the veiled threats of the Kanchenjunga,
Let time pause with the lost pulse
And Death point to the tall sepulchre
Of Mallory's heart and Irvine's bones
Nearest to Heaven upon the Earth.

Under the prismed plume of Everest
Under the cold breast of Chomolungma
Under the white spell of the Himalayas
Beyond the long ladder of the worm
Beyond the curved highway of the hawk
Beyond the need of granite words
To claim their share of grief and glory
Let us sleep in frosty cerements
Forever young, forever at high destiny
Forever hid in wreaths of silence.

Pledged to the cabala of the few
Wedded to the witch of the jeweled fang
True to the lost shrine of the clouds
And noble no less in folly's flag
That lures men into sacrifice,
Let us answer the challenge of a stone
Too high for shadows on the icy cairn—
Not all who climb come down again.

ORIGINAL SIN

Though the spell of sleep
Had settled deep
The child wrinkled her face
With merest trace
Of a frown,
As if her lips had touched the down
Of a peach.
Her hand drew from my reach
And the frown turned into fear
Of something hovering near—
And I felt the wind go by
And heard her whimpering cry
As some unholy thing
Roused the half-dark with its wing.
I signed the cross on him
Circling in the dim
Shadows of the room,
And the child whimpered once more
When the heavy door
Slammed in the gloom.
Fear crawled in the roots of my hair
As I said a prayer
Against the darkness closing round,
And suddenly the sound

Of a vaster wind was heard
And the child stirred,
Grimaced and awoke,
Then she smiled and spoke—
"Where did he go?"
I said I didn't know. . .
The child said, "Yes, you do,
The thing came in with you."

AT THE WAKE

The air is heavy with the musk of sabred flowers
And ballet dancers on the candelabra
Are swaying to soft rhythms of the wind.

My people gather about the pampered dead
Like clansmen in a rowan grove
Huddled around the druid and the flame.
After ten thousand years of swift pursuing
We are not intimate with Death.

Christ on the brazen crucifix
Writhes in new passion in the nervous light
And three old crones are murmuring at their beads.
Men in the kitchen reminisce
Amid the myrrh of nicotine
And laughter blunders through the swinging door
To startle women with a taste for grief.

PSALM FOR THE SORROWING

The cadence of sorrow caresses the heart with a music
Older than Eve in the parched hills older than Eden
Where Cain spelled hate for the world in the bright blood
    of Abel,
It was heard at the courts of Troy by the brooding Cassandra
When the beauty of Helen cursed sons and daughters of Priam.
It's a music that's older than Carthage or fury of Cato,
Older than Jeremiah who grieved for the daughters of Zion.
It was heard by Mary the Virgin who keened on Golgotha's
    shoulder.

The cadence of sorrow is the soft and ultimate rhythm
That soothes the heart long after the wound of the passions.
The red voice of greed shall be choked by the sobbing of
    women,
And the blades of our hate shall dull with the rust of their
    tears,
For these are the prophets who grieve in the prescience of
    sorrow,
Making a balm for our hurt that shall heal us quicker than
    sleep.

RIDING THE DUNES

The squeals of laughter follow every jounce
Along the roller coaster toward land's end.
The tires fat with air grind in the ruts
Except upon the hard beach where the storm
Rubbed out the tracks of yesterday and raised
A driftwood barrier from the boiling surf.
Back of the wind-built mounds the shadows gather
And random tempests spray the sandy ridges
Minting brief rainbows in the levelling sun.
High on the dune a dead tree's topmost branch
Is a bony finger pointing to the sky
Where plovers perch and petrels gather breath.
The gull wings tread the cool electric air
Feathering the light along the blue horizon.

We lift the planks, and ribs, the splintered spars,
The flotsam of a bark, time-trapped and bludgeoned
By knuckles of the gale that stove her sides
To kindling wood and drowned a dozen men.
The lighthouse wakes and blinks along the east
Throwing a lance into the velvet dusk.
The flood tide shows white teeth and runs away,
Returns and steals the footprints from the beach.
Our sand hog snorts and rushes down the shore
Then scampers up the whiskered ridge, eyes glaring
Through the fiction of a thousand little pools

Of grey-green shadows rimmed with rising mist.
The sand cascades from wheels and hurls its spray
On shaggy sides of hummocks stitched together
By needles of the grass these hundred years.

The evening laps the black milk of the wind;
Twin tusks of light rip through the darkened world
Lifting and falling as we climb the knolls.
The silly talk is over; loneliness
Crowds in amid the silence and lies down.
The dunes put on the changing shapes of error
But the eye upon the headland sets the course,
Till we hear the mournful welcome of a buoy,
Then causeway lights, and the halo of the town.
Slowly we shake the mantle of the dunes
And the eternal talk of sea and wind and sand.

THE GRIEF OF ST. MOCHUA*

Mochua wept without restraint
Beside a rowan tree. The saint

Had three friends and they did die—
A cock, a mouse, and a silver fly.

The cock had learned to crow in Latin
And rouse Mochua up at matin.

And if the hermit did not hear
The field mouse nibbled at his ear,

And when his eyes began to falter
The silver fly hummed on the psalter

Moving along the notes Gregorian
To mark the cadences stentorian.

Not rash the sorrow he expended
For the happy days now ended.

The cock grew proud and crowed in Greek
And a verb, irregular, cracked his beak,

The field mouse chancing on a cat
Blessed himself and murmured "scat."

*Pronounced Moc-hoo'a.

94

The fly who marked the psalter scale
Flew headlong into a dewy veil,

Thus Mochua's servants perished
And with them everything he cherished;

And mournfully he took his quill
Making complaint to Columkille.

"Once, I was rich, none can deny,
With a cock, a mouse and a silver fly.

"No king of Eire, Greece, or Rome
Was rich as Mochua in his home

"Of a cloistered grinian* where the gold
Of sun and moon fell on my fold,

"Now poor am I, with pride as scant
As the heart of a wayside mendicant."

Columkille, vexed as a druid oracle,
Hurried to Mochua in his coracle,

And said, "Thou are guilty of heinous sin,
O Mochua, for pride was in

"Your wordly heart. Now may the salt
Of anguish shrive the bitter fault

*Gaelic for sunny grove

95

"And for your penance, search until
You find three gillies on a hill—

"A bird to pluck grain from the eyes
Of a sleepy monk and make him rise,

"And if he slumbers yet, a bee
To rouse him somewhat urgently,

"And for his psalter search the thicket
Until you catch a basso cricket.

"Seeking them, Mochua, pray that I
Find a cock and a mouse and a silver fly."

ARAN TRAGEDY

Black bats from high Dun Aengus
Sweep out of the purple nest
Of clouds stitched by lightning
To a luminous crest.

Anger comes to the islands
Borne by the white-maned steeds
Of Mananaun, who climb the shelves
Of Inishmaan, jibed by the reeds

Of Moorigan, who saw the Danes go down—
Who saw the Spaniards count their loss
Upon the rocks. Colum nor Kieran
Ever put the Holy Cross

Upon her, and her witch's brood.
Last night they swarmed on a cockleshell
Laden with herring and hungry men.
There is no knell—

Only the bitter scream of the wind,
And the keen of women on the barren shore,
Fools are they who go to sea,
Blessed be the fools forevermore.

I

BELTENE
May 1

Fagots from the glen have a fiery sap
Like April blood in the veins of a maiden;
Burn thorny boughs to the woman whose pap
Is heavy with milk and love twice laden.

Pile bramble and bush till the tongues of the fire
Shall speak to the sky that summer is soon,
And Lugh shall walk bright paths of desire
And sire the earth for the birth of June.

May-day for Beltene and the kingdom to feed—
Bless the ocean with fins and the land for bearing,
While embers are warming the restless seed,
Guide nets of the sailors to salmon and herring.

II

LUGHNASAD
August 1

Summer was dying of high fever
But the yellow fields were never
More beautiful than the hour when
Night came out of the sultry glen
Lured by the frenzy and the flame—
Across the stubble and stalk he came
And back to the starlight went he
Hearing the paean of plenty.

III

SAMHAIN
October 31

White-scarfed winds are taunting the black
Banners of darkness, but the yellow skeins
Of the fire make warm shawls for the back.
Men cower when the steeds with wiry manes,
Braided by Lir to an Arctic thong,
Scourge the warrior's shaven cheek.
Add the oak logs now, or the druid's song
Will cease, and a shriller tongue will speak
The prophecy of doom, and the first blight
Of winter will cover the fields in white.

DARK FERGUS OF THE DREAM

Fergus, the senachie, purchased a dream
  And the coin that he tossed to the vendor
Was the full of the moon from an indolent stream,
  Fair tribute to pay for the splendor.

But the dawn was a thief with ankles of light
  And the sun was a plundering vandal,
And dream of the harper faded with night
  At the sound of the dawn's faint sandal.

Then a woman of bronze with high breasts of umber
  Swept down at the margin of dark,
And Fergus drenched deep in the pool of his slumber
  Felt the warmth of her kiss. Then a spark

Of blue fire burned fierce as a rocket
  From the uttermost depths of her mind;
Flame like a meteor danced in each socket
  And Fergus, the harper, was blind.

The woman came back to the shade of the oak
  Where Fergus lay wrapped in his vision
And placed on his shoulder the invisible cloak
  That banished the daylight's derision.

She lit a black candle beside him at dawn
That spread an impenetrable shadow
Shielding his dream till the vandal had gone
From the lake, and the hill and the meadow.

When the omadhawn hammers his drumheads of thunder
And jet clouds roll from the West,
Be sure that Dark Fergus in his raiment of wonder
Sweeps by with a dream in his breast.

LIMERICK LEGEND

A worm of the sea, it was that dug out the Shannon
Gorging his cavernous gut with the moon-sweetened turf,
Until his fangs wore dull on the high rocks of Cavan
And he slithered back to the envious surf.

When the sun rose, the veil of MacDonnell's ghost daughter
Waved in pale fury above the galloping brine
And the torturous pathway quaffed the white-crested water
Like a parched gullet drinking a beaker of wine.

And the sea dropped low by the loss of many a gallon
And the evenings were brightened by spangles of salmon and
    trout
Until the turbulent flood rolled into Lough Allen,
Nor all of your thirsts can ever empty it out.

GRIEF FEAST*

Joy has a banquet of laughter
Where men and women wear masks
To cover the hurt of their hearts,
And they drown the wail of the shee
By spilling the music of fiddles
On the dewy damp of the thatch,
Aye, they trample down bother and sorrow
To the furious whip of the reels
Till death is dancing beside them.

'Tis better to go where grief has a feasting
By the empty bier of a sailor
Who was caught in the net of MacLir.
The faces men wear are their own
And their words are rich in their fewness
And the keening of women awakens
The driftwood flames of the hearth
For salt is the flavor of sorrow
As we feast at the table of grief.

*Suggested by a phrase from a bardic poem.

FOR DEIRDRE

Not all of your warriors sleep in Glasnevin,
Their dust is blown over pampas and veldt,
And the dark woman's song is heard by the Celt
At the doorknob of hell or the postern of heaven.

No deed of Cuchulain is prisoned in granite
But his challenge shall flame on the lips of the Gael,
And the clarion of battle shall lift every sail
Of the rovers who searched for the brink of the planet.

O the continents five and the seas that are seven
Shall beckon forever to the man of Hy Neil,
And every far mountain wears the print of his heel;
Not all of your warriors sleep in Glasnevin.

ANTHONY RAFTERY

A hundred years, Anthony Raftery,* is not so long
When memory is spun from the durable faith of the Gael.
Though your world was the County Mayo, the words of your
   song
May be heard in the West from the blustery tip of Kinsale
To the furious surf that pounds on the shoulders of Tory.
New bards have come to Killeadan with the Sassenach word
To gather your praise to Mayo—and your wreath of glory
For Mary Hynes, and the flirt, Peggy Mitchell. They heard
How the last of the bards with fiddle and aching sockets
Chimed vowels of his rann in a dark and endless duel
With hunger and scorn and the silence of empty pockets
When the hearth of the Gael burnt low for lack of red fuel.
Men had forgotten the grandeur of chieftain and king
Who gave reward that Cormac decreed to the bard,
Ah, Cormac of Tara, where is the poet of Erin to sing
The praise of the ruler whose tongue was ever on guard
Against the chatter of fools, ere the troublous time
When the Latin of Patrick angered the ghost of Oisin?
Chiefs have been crowned or spitted with shame in the rhyme
And the meter more skilled in its weft than the scarf of a queen.
Dan Direacht, when measured by misers of sound has a chime
To awaken the sidhe on the thatch or worry the witches,
And the *Aisling's* a cloak of beauty that sorrow has spun

Last of the Gaelic Bards (died 1835).

From the wool of the cailleach's dark ewe to cover her riches.
Blind bards of the princes have sung of the victories won
By O'Neill and O'Donnell. They told of the fight at the Ford
And pride of Ulster flushed with a rekindled fire.
O'Hussey who hardened his grief to a flashing sword
Has cut our souls to the core lamenting Maguire.
Prince of the poets of Munster, O'Rahilly the proud,
Dreamed of the courts of Clan Cartie who paid him his rank
And walked with want at the heel and his head in a cloud.
O'Bruidar, bitter of tongue, his bitterness drank
When Sarsfield of Lucan left Erin to wager his blood
On the fortunes of France. Ah, shrill was the poet, Mavrone,
Who pitched his song to the wailing of women and stood
On the quays of Limerick after the wild geese had flown!
Eoghan Ruah, whose heart was a furious fountain of song
Flowing sweet and as tart as the angel or rake that possessed
    him—
Old women of Kerry remembering his right and his wrong
Have poured his ranns on the curves of the wind and blest him
And the ghost of O'Sullivan lingers by hedgerow and glen.
Gay Merriman the ribald from Clare, of the midnight court,
Saw daughters of Evall cut whips for the passions of men
And make pursuit of the bachelor a maidenly sport.

The bards of the Gaeltacht are gone, O'Raftery Dall—
Guttered the wick where they toiled with the singable sound
But the fires of the Beal-tinne burn anew at the wall

Of Kilmainham where Pearse and the band of new poets found
The bright Paschal lamp and fed it the oil of their veins.
Oh summon them all—the hero and bard from Glasnevin
To the slope of Slieve Gua and hearken to the golden strains
That shall weave a song for the glory of Terence and Kevin.
Make ready for Feis and for Celigh where harp and the flute
Are commanding the lilt of the tongue and twitch of the toe;
Let Keating the soggarth go sweeten the lips of the mute
With the honey of speech until old melodies flow
From the shadowy silence where Amergin first fashioned his
    breath
For praise to the earth, the ocean and sky, and gave
Bright feathers of song to heroes who bartered with death
And won the height of the heavens for width of the grave.

CORMAC MAC AIRT

Wisdom is a gift to crown all virtues,
For who can be wise if he is not just;
And who can be just if he has not mercy
And mercy's a gift that is spurned by the fool.

Cormac, grandson of Conn, of the Battles,
The salmon fed you the spawn of his mind,
And you drank the brew of the oak sap and rowan,
And humbled the druids when you fashioned thought.

Envy to Carberry who sat at your counsel
With ears like leaves to capture the dew;
Your words were slaves to a heavier burden
Than ever a Brehon could yoke to his tongue.

Silence was a woman to soothe quiet hours,
As stars leaned down to your reach for the sky,
But the five roads to Tara were curving with music
When the bards and harpers were called to the Feis.

Lugh blest your vision with light in the darkness—
In the darkness of men you threw rowan flares,
While the boaster stumbled on pride that was broken,
And liars winced on the edges of truth.

SWAN CURSE

Pity you Phelim Quinn of the bogs and the fidgety finger
That burned a thunderous hole in the sagging web of the dark.
Years rust on your gun, but the sound of death shall linger
Till the heavier clap of doom. Swifter than prayer the spark
Of evil that pierced the soggy stillness and the breast of a swan.
How oft the wanton pair of us saw the pale bird fetching
A shadowy meaning from sedge and shallow to press on
The moon for an instant of awe and silence, or stretching
An arrowy neck to the salt winds jostling over the marsh.

Pity you twice, O bard of the maimed and muted tongue;
The echo of hate in the glen of the mist is hollow and harsh.
Once sang you of Children of Lir bewitched by envy to young
White swans, whose pinions were caught in the icy crest of the
    Moyle,
Aye, bound as the wings of your song are bound this wintry
    weather;
And parched is your soul tonight, as the angry scar on the soil
Where fell God's grace from the broken sky, with a bloody
    feather.

THE GREY MACHA

Down from Slieve Gullion the Grey Macha races
   His wide nostrils charging the valley with fog.
And around the high mound of Dun Dalgan he paces
   To the bellow of kine and the squeal of the hog.

On the lips of the Boyne is the print of his hoof,
   Aye, to the groves of Maeve and her lover;
Dark Moorigan hears him stamp on her roof
   In the field where he found the honey-dipped clover,

His whinnying catches the shroud of the wind
   As he finds the gash of a chariot wheel,
Wide as a ditch that might shelter a hind,
   And deep as a grave for thieves of Aileel.

But where is the shield no storm ever darkens
   And the tooth of the Gae-Bolg thirsty for blood,
"Cuchulain, Cuchulain?" The Grey Macha hearkens
   And hears but the moaning of Lir in his flood.

Back to Slieve Gullion, the Grey Macha is flying
   And the fire of fury streaks out of his mane;
The oak trees are writhing, the bittern is crying,
   The son of Sualtam shall not come again.

IN MEMORIAM

Five Irish lads stood tiptoe on the prairie
Stared over the plumed high corn of Iowa
And saw the blue Pacific lap the dusk,
And where the sky sloped down on the winter wheat
They watched the wind sweep through the green shoal water
And their hearts beat faster with the distant rumble
In the dark flotillas of the thunderheads.

II

Six centuries long the Sullivans of Kerry
Have looked to the west from bastions of Bearehaven,
Looked through the mists of Dingle toward the Blaskets
Hugging the horizon like great men-of-war,
Looked through the Gulf Stream's breath beyond the pennons
Of Spanish ships with wine and spice for Galway,
Looked for the land of youth and the land of promise
And they sailed west with the faith and songs of Kerry
Landing where whim of wind and commerce brought them,
Boston, New York, Penn's city on the Bay,
Savannah, Charleston, the diked-up Creole city.
Hewers of wood and breakers of land, they gouged
The waterways across New York, New Jersey,
Built plank roads through the swamps, and bridged the rivers,
Drove spikes with rhythm of the panting engine

And caught the dreams of empire in their hands.
Somewhere along the road their hearts made anchor
On prairie land, and sons and daughters came
With the blueness of deep water in their eyes.

III

If oil will soothe the ferment of the ocean
A drop of blood will bring the sea to boil
And spread the rancor till all shores are stained
By the wrack that purges from the hearts of men.
December Seven. The little men of Nippon
Feathered like falcons with unhooded eyes
Fall on Pearl Harbor drugged in Sunday slumber,
And make the stain that honor must erase.
The sons of Kerrymen rush to the quarrel
Out of the midlands and their pulse is tuned
To tides of tempest though they've seen no ship
Save the argosies that drift across the moon.

IV

Five Sullivans from Iowa go forth to battle
Linked arm in arm, and make the willing bargain,
Win all, lose all, they take the cruiser *Juneau*
Which burrows southward through the dangerous isles
And plumbless depths and distance of blue water,
The old mirage of the winter wheat come true.

The Jap and Yank played many a game of tag
Through mist and rain, and coral reef and atoll,
But the Jap was *it* when the hide-and-seek was ended
And eight and twenty keels of the mute Mikado
Plummeted down three miles with seams wide open.
Nine Yankee craft went under, one the *Juneau,*
Her skin of steel ripped open but the mouths
Of her long guns spat flame across the water
Till water chilled their gullets with a hiss
Of fury, and they spoke no more in anger.

V

Sing out the paean for the Yankee valor
With foeman vanquished and with shame avenged
But brothers five who came from Iowa
Will look no more on wind in the winter wheat
Nor hear the dry husks rustle in the Autumn;
They sleep with friend and enemy below
The curved blue arches of the Coral Sea.
Though sons of Kerry sail on every ocean
The sea's the sea the blessed wide world over,
And the Gael who steers by the shadow of the gull,
With O'Bruidar the Rogue and Brendan the saintly rover,
Hears the heavenly horn that summons sailors home.

I, MICHAELANGELO

I

Born at Caprese near the Arno's tide
I haunt the half-hewn blocks Carrara gave
My hands to shape for pope, and prince and knave
Till an old man fell beneath the whip of pride.
Let Rome and Florence taunt the soul denied
A saint's serene, I seek the quarry cave
And wrestle stone, the master and the slave,
And search the curve of meaning lost inside.

God touched the clay to flesh. I touched the stone
With fire. The sibyls on the Sistine ceiling
Whisper the song that Adam heard alone
And bid me send the sons of Adam reeling
With anger of the mallet to atone
For sins against the Word, and Love's sweet healing.

The shadows crowd around me in an arc
Of a plaster heaven where the paint and lime
Are matted in my beard. I yearn to climb
The scaffold to the stars beyond the dark
And hear the prophets' voices, see the spark
Of angry eyes burn through Creation's grime
Like beacons on the rim of canceled time
And watch the meteors make their warning mark.

Above me sit the prophets Jeremiah,
Isaiah, Joel, Ezekiel, who wrung
Their hands in pity as my muscles pained
Supine upon the planks while the Messiah
Was promised by the sibyls with a tongue
Of gentle treason as Zeus' sceptre waned.

III

Grant me the sword of Michael to unfrock
The cowled blue mountains with the protean scheme
That once I saw beyond the chisel's gleam
When the eye of Lucifer burned through the block
Of stubborn dust, and my two fists shall mock
The shape of evil straining to blaspheme.
The Power is mine; caught from a heavenly beam
And prisoned in the pulsing vein of rock.

Remember David, hewn of a single stone,
Within whose gaze the everlasting fire
Would stun Goliath without a favored sling;
Turn ye to Moses, prophet of flesh and bone;
Zeus shrinks before the Jew whose lips inspire
The arid cliff to answer with a spring.

IV

I strove in marble, but I grieved in song;
My hammer won or lost the public wage,
But poems were whispered ointment to assuage
The heart tormented by a secret prong;
Dark were the years when large and little wrong
Festered in malice to enormous rage.
I asked for solace on the poet's page
And held the tranquil moment, not for long.

Men publish once in marble, never more.
The sculptor dare not rouse the holy thing
He wakened once with chatter of the maul;
No echoes roll from the Ligurian shore
Of steel on stone, but words of Dante ring
Over the world as leaders rise and fall.

V

I wrestled failure; San Lorenzo's shrine
Bears testimony, eloquent if mute.
The tomb of Julius, maimed with long dispute,
Loses the grandeur of the dawn's design.
The shattered figures, there were nine times nine,
Rise from the heap of shards beneath the boot
And charge my guilty hand. The speckled fruit
Rots at Bargello and the fault is mine.

Who has not stared upon the Laocoön
Nor knows the frenzy of a soul enchained?
Through all the fourscore of my fevered years
My vision burned through darkness like a sun
And in the end the wings of darkness stained
The sunset hour in a shroud of fears.

VI

Fame was a fickle lady I met oft
Coming and going on the path to Rome;
She smiled at me beneath her Tuscan comb
Within Lorenzo's garth, holding aloft
My faun grown swiftly old beneath the soft
Autumnal moon. But querulous as a gnome
That guards Carrara's caverns I went home
To sulk in Florence when my lady scoffed.

She kept my heart in anguish. At a whim
She chose young Raphael. I saw her hold
Him for the Pope's high favor, fondling him
As once she favored me, and turning cold
To Leonardo, her shrewd paradigm.
I worried less about her, growing old.

I was enslaved to Envy in my prime;
I met him when Bramante spurred the Pope
To strip the pagan heart of Rome. My hope
Of hearing echoes of the Aegean rhyme
Upon Tyrrhenean littoral through all time
Dimmed like a foolish dream. A misanthrope
Wandered in anguish by Carrara's slope
Where the knave Bramante plagued him with a smile.

My heart grew poor from borrowed discontent.
Envy, the vintner, sold a bitter wine
And made my tongue his debtor. Hatred spent
My years of treasure by the evil vine;
"Thou fool," a voice said and the voice was mine,
But neither Time nor Envy would relent.

VIII

I modeled snow for the Medici's delight
And Piero is remembered with the snow
That hardened once when Michaelangelo
Challenged the sun with all of winter's might.
Rude Bandenelli left the chisel's blight
Upon the marble. Better the hammer blow
Had fallen on a block of ice than show
Such folly to the centuries of light.

Men threw their malice at me like a ball
Of snow, and I returned it made of ice,
And some have tossed the flowers of a friend
Like traders on the mart, I spurned them all
Except the praise that came without a price,
I took these words beyond the season's end.

IX

If I were less than noble, having learned
That poisoned words were daggers at my back,
Or if my temper showed a peasant's lack
Of grace to princely foemen, I have spurned
No challenge from the sage or fool, nor turned
The cheek nor heel from any man's attack,
I gave no room to guile within my pack;
Only for love and hatred fairly earned.

DaVinci's eyes showed fire when I told him
His bronze was poorly cast. Pope Julius saw
My pride rise higher than a pontiff's nose,
But speak no ill of Julius, I'll uphold him,
He was a large man, making plain the flaw
Of Adam's nature in his godly clothes.

X

Nature I served the lesser. Yea, I knew
The color of the bird-wing and the name
Of many stars before the Arabs came
With signs for the pin pricks in the purple hue
Of evening. What had heathen seers to do
With making stars, and would they share the blame
If the returning orb were not the same,
Or if the course in the heavens were not true?

I dealt with Godhead. Nature can defend
Herself in trivial aspects of the season,
The winds of winter, and the breath of spring.
I celebrate Beginnings and the End
Of men and angels in their days of treason,
Let others paint the cloud, the leaf, the wing.

My certainty of will came from the breast
Of a quarry matron from whose paps I drank,
The liquid marble. Till time's end I'll thank
Her for the strength of hands that took the best
Carrara had to offer. In the quest
To mirror hearts of men upon the blank
White face of stone my courage never shrank
But found the blood and sinew for the test.

The palette holds the art of one dimension;
I grudge the years I served the lesser shrine
Upon the scaffold sore of heart and bone.
I am the sculptor. That was fate's intention
When milk of Settignano gave me spine
To take the breadth, and length and depth of stone.

XII

Like Hercules I strained beneath the dome
Where popes have reigned and peasants have been crowned
With Peter's jeweled diadem. Each pound
Pressed on me like a page out of the tome
Of Judgment as I walked the streets of Rome.
Blame to Sangallo, then. The hollow sound
Of his tall columns echoed to the ground
With fraud and folly in St. Peter's home.

Atlas who walked away in anger saw his world
Roll down the blue vast of the sky unharmed;
But had I shirked the devils would have hurled
The faith-hewn rock of Peter down in rubble.
My hammers said "Thou cheat," and Rome alarmed
Dispersed the knaves who set their snares of trouble.

XIII

The Pietà was carved in two sad years
When mischief roamed the world on cloven feet
And Savonarola felt the fagot's heat
Without the quenching miracle of tears.
Rumors of war and treason plagued our ears
As men went gathering whispers in the street,
Then San Dionige's cardinal dropped the sheet
And the cry of pity drowned ten thousand fears.

Love was the summons from the lips of sorrow
As the Mother took the burden of the Cross,
God's generous payment for the sinner's debt,
But sadder still were the omens for the morrow
When Rome would meet a century of loss
And northern Christendom would slip the net.

Torrigiano's fist became a mace
To change my outward features, inner mien.
I walked head downward fearing to be seen
By urchins who would mock a broken face.
I sought no comely maiden to embrace
But held the shield of ugliness between
My heart and the caress of Eve. The clean
And chill curve of the marble took her place.

I sketched the blemish once as stones turned colder
Looking askew at the image in the glass
Daring a furtive glance across my shoulder
As if I sensed a duke or knave would pass,
But it was only Time and I grew bolder
Saying, "Death mends all scars. It always has."

If young men find a fever in the blood
Lit by the candle of a maiden's glances,
My twisted face invited no sweet lances
But shielded me from evil and from good
Within the will of woman. When the rude
Impulses chilled, a widow took her chances
And held her candle for my shrewd advances—
What matters then—pursuer or pursued?

Her whitened words dripped as a blessed balm
Upon the scars of time's unending duel
With paint and stone, and made the evening path
A brighter way to walk. Vittoria's calm
Sweet words at going home destroyed the cruel
Device of death, and turned aside his wrath.

Prisoner of light and shadow, I must stand
Upon the lichened quarry ridge and keep
The vigil for the tortured things that sleep
Within Carrara's caves. They wait my hand
In vain to give the chisel's sharp command.
Good cancels evil as the centuries creep
Across Lorenzo's garden, but the women weep
Amidst the rubble of our punished land.

If I have failed, I fail with every man
Who dares beyond his depth. I heard Dawn sing
And seized her rhythms like a thief unbidden
Holding the shapes for all the world to scan
And then too late I felt the Darkness cling
To stones wherein all Heaven's themes are hidden.